UNDERSTANDING the SECRET of PREVAILING PRAYER

Rev Franklin N Abazie

Understanding the Secret of Prevailing Prayer

Copyright © 2014 by Rev Franklin N Abazie

All rights reserved. This book or any portion thereof may not be reproduced or used in any manner whatsoever without the express written permission of the publisher, except for the use of brief quotations in a book review. All Bible quotes are from King James Version and others as noted.

Published by:

F N Abazie Publishing House

a.k.a *Empowerment Bookstore*

Psalms 26:7 - That I may publish with the voice of thanksgiving, and tell of all thy wondrous works.

To order additional copies, wholesale or bookings,
Church Office: (973) 372-7518
33 Schley Street • Newark, NJ 07112
email: pastorfranknto@yahoo.com
www.fnabaziepublishinghouse.org

www.fnabaziehealingministries.org

Cover Design: www.AngelPrints.net

First Printing, 2014 in the USA
by Whole Without A Crack Publications
www.WWACPSelfPublishing.net

Second Printing, 2015 in the USA
by Ingram Spark

ACKNOWLEDGMENT

I would like to take this opportunity to acknowledge and thank Rev. Dr. David Jefferson, Sr. for the great impact and influence he has had over my life. The Holy Spirit used Rev. Dr. David Jefferson's classical message of this great day, March 28th 1999, first to convict me to repent. Then I gave my life to the Lord Jesus. Secondly it confirmed the gift and calling of God over my life. The Holy Spirit used this classical message to bring me into preaching the gospel of Jesus Christ.

By the grace of God I was called to revive the healing & miracle ministry of Jesus Christ of Nazareth by divine election, and not by human selection. It pleased the Lord to separate me and use me as a vessel to write this prayer book as a Healing Evangelist by His grace.

I would also like to thank all of my spiritual mentors, especially Bishop David Oyedepo and Pastor David Ibiyeomie, both of whom the Lord used greatly first to encourage me in my ministry work. The Lord also used this great men of God for me to take a bold step towards writing spiritual literature. To date, I have written a lot books by the grace of God. Although I have watched almost every video message of Dr. David Oyedepo, I have listened and watched more video and audio messages of my great mentors who went to glory more than I have read books of my living mentors therefore. I would also like to mention the blessed memory of my departed mentors who went to be with the Lord. May their souls rest in perfect glory: Oral Roberts and Papa Kenneth E Hagin.

Finally I give Special thanks to God and my lovely wife and children for bringing this book into a reality. To God lone be all the Glory.

TABLE OF CONTENTS

Chapter 1
The Prayer of Faith ... 13

Chapter 2
The Power of Meditation ... 23

Chapter 3
The Power of Patience & Endurance ... 31

Chapter 4
The Voice of Thanksgiving ... 35

Chapter 5
The Power of Praise ... 39

Prayer of Salvation ... 43

About the Author ... 46

THE MANDATE OF THE COMMISSION

"THE MOMENT IS DUE TO IMPACT YOUR WORLD THROUGH THE REVIVAL OF THE HEALING & MIRACLE MINISTRY OF JESUS CHRIST OF NAZARETH. I AM SENDING YOU TO RESTORE HEALTH UNTO THEE AND I WILL HEAL THEE OF THY WOUNDS. SAID THE LORD OF HOST"

Arms of the Commission

1) F N Abazie Ministries: Miracle of God Healing Church (Miracle Chapel Intl)

2) F N Abazie TV Ministries: Global Television Ministry Outreach

3) F N Abazie Radio Ministries: Radio Broadcasting Outreach

4) F N Abazie Publishing House: Book Publication

5) F N Abazie Bible School: also called Word of Healing Bible School (W.O.H.B.S)

6) F N Abazie Evangelistic Ass: Miracle of God Ministries: Global Crusade

7) Empowerment Bookstore: Book distribution

8) F N Abazie Helping Hands: Meeting the help of the needy world wide

9) F N Abazie Disaster Recovery Mission: Global Disaster Recovery

10) F N Abazie Prison Ministry: Prison Ministry for all convicts "Second chance

Some of our ministry arms are waiting the appointed time to commence.

FOREWORD

Rev. Franklin N Abazie is a dynamic man of prayer. I have come to know this humble man of God as a man of prayer, with unlimited insight and understanding of the strategies and tactics of Prevailing Prayers. His life and ministry is a life and ministry of prayer. This book is a must read!!

I recommend you get a copy of this book for your edification and comfort. His books, Understanding the Secret of the Man God Uses and Understanding the Secret of Prevailing Prayers, will equip and build any man or woman of God interested in following divine guidance and divine leading.

I thank God for knowing this humble servant of God. He has been immensely of a great blessing. I pray and recommend this book to every one in the household of God.

Thanks,
Pastor Isaac Conney
Christ Gospel Ministry - Newark, NJ USA

INTRODUCTION

In this end time, prayer is of utmost importance; it is a device used to wage effective war against the wiles and schemes of the devil. Regrettably, so many people have neglected and forgotten the power of prayer. In the kingdom of God, no man can go far without a precise understanding of what it takes to prevail in prayer. I have come to a conclusion that prevailing prayers are the prayers that defeats and humiliates the enemy.

Prayer is vital and of utmost importance in the life of the believer. Perhaps you have heard and read many books and brochures about prayer, but humble your mind and read what the Holy Ghost is breathing in this book.

I admonish you read this book without any biased mind-set nor conflict of interest. Please, throw down your how-to techniques and follow me as I reveal to you what the Holy Ghost is saying about prevailing prayers.

According to the principles of the Master Jesus, and the demands of the disciples, we must learn how to pray, and further more we must understand how to pray. Therefore, come with me as I reveal to you the mysteries of prevailing prayer. I will answer your most bugging questions about prayers as we proceeds.

What is Prayer?

Prayer is communication to your Heavenly Father. It is speaking and listening to God. That is-communicating to the Almighty God, with reverence and respect, as supreme and sovereign over all the affairs of life and every territory on the planet. Prayer is making supplication and requests unto God to visit man's affairs in the earth realm. It is provoking the hand of God to move and shift things positively that will benefit you. Prayer is asking God, from His divinity perspective, to visit humanity with concrete and unquestionable results. Prayer is provoking God to send angelic help to rescue man from frustration, challenges and obstacles. Please follow me as I hit on the subject of prevailing prayer. I pray, May the God of Jacob visit you. Amen

Luke 11:1-4

And it came to pass, that, as he was praying in a certain place, when he ceased, one of his disciples said unto him, Lord, teach us to pray, as John also taught his disciples.

And he said unto them, When ye pray, say, Our Father which art in heaven, Hallowed be thy name. Thy kingdom come. Thy will be done, as in heaven, so in earth. Give us day by day our daily bread. And forgive us our sins; for we also forgive every one that is indebted to us. And lead us not into temptation; but deliver us from evil.

1

The Mystery of Faith

James 5:15
And the prayer of faith shall save the sick, and the Lord shall raise him up; and if he have committed sins, they shall be forgiven him.

Regardless of your faith, any prayer of faith covers all other types of intercessory, deliverance and prophetic prayers. It will make sense as I further explain it. It is faith that carries your spoken words into the throne room of the Father Almighty. Therefore faith is your access key to open and unlock the mysteries that are coded in prayers .When the bible said without faith you cannot please God (Hebrews 11:6). This literally means attention cannot be given to any uttered words in prayers that is not mixed with faith. Faith is the energy that fuel prayers, it is the catalyst upon which divine interventions are provoked. When the bible said that the prayers of faith shall save the sick, it is important here to note the following: 1) That faith guarantees divine healing. 2) That faith brings restoration, 3) That faith provokes the advocate-Jesus to rise up on your defense.

The prayer of faith must be heart

born, heart felt, it must generate from the heart. This I mean; scripture teaches that a heartfelt prayer availed much anyway! This prayer must be communicated unto God with reverence, fear sincerity, humility and respect.

Matthew 6:6
But thou, when thou prayest, enter into thy closet, and when thou hast shut thy door, pray to thy Father which is in secret; and thy Father which seeth in secret shall reward thee openly.

The prayer of faith must be offered on the plat form of conviction; this I mean that your prayers must be backed with genuine action plans. There must be an active action plan in your life coupled with some healthy believe system. Your prayers must be mixed with faith to prevail.

Mark 11:24
Therefore I say unto you, What things so-ever ye desire, when ye pray, believe that ye receive them, and ye shall have them.

After you have spoken out what you want God to do for your life in prayers, you must follow it up by consciously developing an actions plan that will guarantee the desired results. By this I mean your mouth and heart must be in agreement. Whatsoever you are saying from your mouth must be what your heart has conceived with a burning passion. As long as you pray out of conviction it will commit and provoke the integrity of God to prevail in your life.

Psalms 37:5
Commit thy way unto the LORD; trust also in him; and he shall bring it to pass.

The prayer of faith secures heaven's attention. It is the prayer of faith that arrests angelic hosts for your quick intervention. When you pray, God hears you, and sends His angels to rescue and deliver you. A meticulous examination of Daniel 10:12 will prove my argument to be correct. From the first day Daniel prayed, angels were available to intervene on his request.

Daniel 10:12
Then said he unto me, Fear not, Daniel: for from the first day that thou didst set thine

heart to understand, and to chasten thyself before thy God, thy words were heard, and I am come for thy words.

Mark 11:23
For verily I say unto you, That whosoever shall say unto this mountain, Be thou removed, and be thou cast into the sea; and shall not doubt in his heart, but shall believe that those things which he saith shall come to pass; he shall have whatsoever he saith.

The prayer of faith must be consciously implemented and executed on the platform of conviction, commitment, confidence and understanding. In the school of faith, it is a law to pray without wavering.

James 1:6
But let him ask in faith, nothing wavering. For he that wavereth is like a wave of the sea driven with the wind and tossed. No man can speak to any mountain, obstacle and challenge without inner strength. In my own definition inner strength is total conviction and confidence in God.

Until you develop confidence when you pray, fear and doubt is permitted to prevail in your life. I want you to examine this scripture:

1 John 5:14-15
And this is the confidence that we have in him, that, if we ask any thing according to his will, he heareth us: And if we know that he hear us, whatsoever we ask, we know that we have the petitions that we desired of him

This is what Jesus said in John 14:13-14: *And whatsoever ye shall ask in my name, that will I do, that the Father may be glorified in the Son. If ye shall ask any thing in my name, I will do it.*

Despite the provision of the above scripture, many believers in the faith pray without the understanding of the basic techniques and tactics to prevail. They are therefore violating the basic principles and fundamental guidelines provided by the Master Jesus. The reason many people have not prevailed in prayer is because they pray without conviction and understanding. Jesus warned and admonished us not to be like the hypocrites who love to pray standing in the synagogues and in the corners of the streets that they may be seen of men.

Matthew 6:5
And when thou prayest, thou shalt not be as the hypocrites are: for they love to pray standing in the synagogues and in the corners of the streets, that they may be seen of men. Verily I say unto you, They have their reward.

Matthew 7:7-8
Ask, and it shall be given you; seek, and ye shall find; knock, and it shall be opened unto you: For every one that asketh receiveth; and he that seeketh findeth; and to him that knocketh it shall be opened.

Now, with the above scripture, before I continue, I want you to say this prayer with violent faith: First repent of any known sin in your life. Accept and acknowledged the Lord Jesus as the Lord of your life. Now, from the heavenly perspective repeat these prayers out loud:

1) I release myself from the captivity of any

hindering spirit, in the name of Jesus
2) I bind principalities and powers, in the name of Jesus.
3) I pronounce the blood of Jesus over everything that concerns me, in Jesus' name.
4) Spirit of the Living God, transform and translate my life even, as I read this prayer booklet, in the name of Jesus.
5) Holy Ghost fire, burn and paralyze everything that is oppressing and torturing me, in the mighty name of Jesus.
6) Power of God, prove yourself mighty against all fetish and diabolic powers, in the name of Jesus.
7) I take authority over the air waves, the sea, land and region of the marine kingdom, in the name of Jesus
8) Blood of Jesus, bring a speedy turn around in my life, in the mighty name of Jesus.
9) Fire of God, burn every arrow sent against me, in the name of Jesus.
10) I dismiss and nullify all agreements with witchcraft covens programed against my life, future, ministry and family, in the name of Jesus.
11) Blood of Jesus, burn all family idols

waging war against my rising, in the name of Jesus.

12) I uproot and terminate all assignments of the wizard over my life, in the name of Jesus.
13) I dismiss all devices programed for my demise, in the name of Jesus.
14) Power of God, bring to pass my desired change, in the name of Jesus.
15) Fire of God, catapult me to the pinnacle of my life, in the name of Jesus.
16) Breakthrough power, visit me with speed, in the name of Jesus.
17) Finger of God, deliver me from the mouth of the devourer, in the name of Jesus
18) I stop every foundational power depositing sickness and disease in my body, in the name of Jesus.
19) Spirit of God, deliver my family from the stronghold of all foundational family powers, in the name of Jesus.
20) Blood of Jesus, break the stronghold of demonic witches and territorial powers caging my destiny, in the name of Jesus.

After saying these short powerful prayers, take time and mediate on Psalms 35,

REV FRANKLIN N. ABAZIE 21

55, 59, and 91. Repeat these prayer points as you desire and watch the hand of God move in your direction.

As I conclude this chapter about the prayer of faith, I want to end by giving you the keys and basic qualities that must be present for the prayer of faith to prevail over every affair of your life:

1) The prayer of faith must be offered in secret. (Matthew 6:6, Psalms 91:1)
2) The prayer of faith must be offered from a repented heart. (Psalm 51:3)
3) The prayer of faith must be pure. (Titus 1:15)
4) The prayer of faith must be backed with expectation. (Romans 8:19)
5) The prayer of faith must be genuine and sincere. (John 8:32,36)
6) The prayer of faith must be offence free. (Matthew 17:1-2)
7) The prayer of faith must be born out of love for God. (1 John 4:16)
8) The prayer of faith must be implemented with a genuine action plan.

2

The Power of Meditation

Genesis 24:63
"And Isaac went out to meditate in the field at the eventide; and he lifted up his eyes, and saw, and behold, the camels were coming."

Although the medical community has proven, with facts and statistics, the benefits of meditation, regrettably a lot of believers who pray and fast every day have neglected and dismissed the importance of meditation. They are therefore perpetually wandering in the wilderness of ignorance. David said, in Psalms 119:99, I have more understanding than all my teachers: for thy testimonies are my meditation. Let me put it in my own way: the testimony of the medical science is the meditation of the believers. I want you to pay close attention to this chapter. The power of meditation cannot be over emphasized. Meditation can only be clearly understood on the platform of understanding. The power of mediation will only produce results on the platform of quietness and confidence.

Isaiah 30:15
in quietness and in confidence shall be your strength.

Actually, the above scripture is revealing that it is only in quietness and confidence that meditation produces the desired result.

What does it mean to practice meditation?

I want you to understand me here very clearly; to practice meditation means creating quiet time in solitude. The Master Jesus left His disciples and went to pray in a quiet place. It was during the meditation of that prayer that Jesus gained confidence and requested that the cup pass from him.

Matthew 26:36-39

Then cometh Jesus with them unto a place called Gethsemane, and saith unto the disciples, Sit ye here, while I go and pray yonder. And he took with him Peter and the two sons of Zebedee, and began to be sorrowful and very heavy. Then saith he unto them, My soul is exceeding sorrowful, even unto death: tarry ye here, and watch with me. And he went a little farther, and fell on his face, and prayed, saying, O my Father, if it be possible, let this cup pass from me: nevertheless not as I will, but as thou wilt.

Although fasting will humble your flesh, it is meditation that will grant you the confidence, boldness and faith to do the will of God. Furthermore, it is meditation that will produce and deliver the right word. Job 6:25 says, *"How forcible are the right words."* Therefore, it is importance to your spiritual life as a believer that, when you pray and communicate to God, you make room for meditation; create time to ponder and wonder, reflect, think and listen to what the Holy Ghost is saying to your situation. No matter how deep you find yourself in a predicament, there is a way out for you; there is a way up and forward for you. The bible commanded us to be still and know that He is God.

Psalms 46:10
…Be still and know that I am God.

Habakkuk 2:1
I will stand upon my watch, and set me upon the tower, and will watch to see what he will say unto me, and what I shall answer when I am reproved.

Until you condition and set yourself

on the tower to watch and see what God will say to you, you are not a candidate to prevail in prayer. Once you are in prayer with God, understand that it is a two way communication channel. When you speak and make your request, intercession, supplications, create time to mediate, to reflect, think and listen to what God will say. You must allow God to talk back to you. You see, God is Spirit. It is scripturally proven that the Holy Spirit communicates back to you in a small still voice (1 Kings 19:11-12). The power of meditation is hidden in your ability to listen attentively to what the Holy Ghost is saying in response to your request.

Proverbs 4:20
My son, attend to my words; incline thine ear unto my sayings. Let them not depart from thine eyes; keep them in the midst of thine heart. For they are life unto those that find them, and health to all their flesh. Keep thy heart with all diligence; for out of it are the issues of life.

Now, Let us examine the principles and fundamental requirements for mediation to produce results.

> Briefly, let's look at the foundational pillars for meditation to prevail

1) ***You must repent of your sins***: Sin hinders all forms of prayer. It hides the face of God from you (Isaiah 59:1-2). The bible says that God does not hear sinners (John 9:31). It is mandatory. You must come out of sin and give your life to Jesus Christ (Romans 3:23, 6:23). No amount of meditation will produce any genuine results as long as sin is in your life (Acts 3:19, Luke 13:5, 2 Peter 3:9). Until sin is cast out, meditation will not prevail . David said, "thy word have I hid in mine heart that I might not sin against thee." Sin is a hindrance to prevail in prayers, furthermore, it is a device of the devil to steal and hide your blessings. The word says, "he that committed sin is of the devil" (1 John 3:7). As long as sin is prevailing in your life, your meditation will only produce condemnation, guilt and diabolic results to the advantage of the devil. Therefore, I admonish you to come out of sin and seek the face of the Lord for evermore.

2) ***You must establish a relationship***: Until you establish a genuine relationship with the Lord Jesus, you will never enjoy effective communication with Him or its benefits. God is a loving Father and not a wicked judge; God is not willing for any to perish. Until you receive Him, you will never have the power to become a son, in the Kingdom of God(John 1:12): "But as many as received him, to them gave he power to become the sons of God, even to them that believe on his name." This I mean that you must repent of your sins and accept the Lord Jesus as your personal Lord and Savior (See John 3:3-7, 16, 2 Peter 3:9).

3) ***Practice Righteousness***: Meditation in prayer will prevail once righteousness is in place. Nothing can stop your prayers from generating concrete and unquestionable results as long as you practice righteousness. Listen to me, Jesus died for your sins (1 Corinthians 15:3). "He made us righteous with God" (2 Corinthians 5:21). Jesus Christ is the mediator of the new covenant (Hebrew 12:24) who has reconciled us to the Father (Colossians

1:18-21). Child of God, understand that no matter the affliction and the invasion of the devil, the Lord will deliver you from all the devices of the devil (Psalms 34:19). 1 Peter 3:13 says, "and who is he that will harm you, if ye be followers of that which is good." Ecclesiastes 8:5 says, "whoso keepeth the commandment shall feel no evil thing." Righteousness will bring ease and make mediation effective. I want you to put all these into practice and you watch how quickly your prayers will be answered.

Next, pray the following prayer points:

PRAYER TO BREAK THE CURSE OF LIFE
Be sincere with yourself as you pray. Say, "In the name of Jesus, I confess and repent of the sins and iniquities of my parents (you can name it if you know it -please mention it here from idol worship, ancestral spirit worship to worship of the dead and grandparents worship).

In the name of Jesus, and by the power of His blood, I now renounce, break asunder all linking cords of iniquity and generational curses I inherited from my parents, grandparents and all other ancestors. I break and nullify it, in Jesus' name.

1) Heavenly Father, visit my life with speed for good, in the name of Jesus.
2) My prayers must receive speedy answers, in the name of Jesus.
3) No weapon fashioned against me shall prosper, in Jesus' name.
4) I silence and cancel all the wiles and schemes of the devil against my life.
5) Blood of Jesus, harken unto the voice of my understanding.
6) Holy Ghost fire, turn every curse against me into a blessing, in the name of Jesus
7) Holy Ghost fire, grant me the desires of my heart, in the name of Jesus.
8) Power of God, dominate the enemies of my life, in the name of Jesus.
9) Hand of God, let your will be done in my life according to your design over my life, in Jesus' name
10) Thank you Lord, in Jesus' name, Amen.

The Power of Patience & Endurance

Hebrews 10:36
"For ye have need of patience, that after ye have done the will of God, ye might receive the promise."

It is significant that when you pray, you believe that you receive (Mark 11:24). I want you to also know it is vital that when you pray, you make room for patience and endurance. God is a God of time and seasons and, at the appointed time, He will bring to pass His good word concerning you. It is against spiritual principles for anyone to pray and then turn around to despise the same words he uttered in prayer. Ecclesiastes 5:6 says, Suffer not thy mouth to cause thy flesh to sin; neither say thou before the angel, that it was an error: wherefore should God be angry at thy voice, and destroy the work of thine hands?

Child of God, form a habit of waiting on the Lord. You do not only wait on the Lord by fasting, but also by exercising patience and endurance. Abraham waited for Isaac to be born and Hannah waited for Samuel to be born. Isaac, Jacob, Rebecca and Rachel were great men and women of the faith who waited an average of 20 - 25 years for their prayers and heart's desire to be fulfilled. I have come to a conclusion about patience and endurance; I call it long-suffering. I want you to know this truth about long-suffering: it is the fruit of the Spirit (Galatians 5:22). Long-suffering is an important characteristic of all prevailing prayers.

Instant gratification or instant response in prayers can be misinterpreted and misrepresented. Oftentimes so many theological critics term it as a wrong doctrine. Many people have flooded the Pentecostal faith in search of instant miracles, signs and wonders. I do not disagree with the instant healing and miracles of God. I love it because it humbles the pride of the heathen and brings conviction to pagans and those of the other faith; However instant gratification and instant miracles win souls for Christ; Nevertheless, with respect to prevailing prayer, it is commanded you learn to be patient by practicing endurance.

Acts 12:5 says, *but prayer was made*

without ceasing of the church unto God for him. In the above scripture, the church exercised patience and endurance by praying without ceasing until the angel of God rescued Peter from the prison. This was the manifestation of the power of patience and endurance. The word says, in Mark 13:13, *but he that shall endure unto the end, the same shall be saved.* Many people pray, but with no genuine results because they cast away their confidence and despise their own genuine prayers by impatience.

Hebrew 10:35-36
Cast not away therefore your confidence, which hath great recompense of reward. For ye have need of patience, that, after ye have done the will of God, ye might receive the promise.

Acts 6:4
But we will give ourselves continually to prayer, and to the ministry of the word.

The first church prevailed in prayer. As long as constant and continual prayers are bombarding the host of Heaven, the Holy Ghost has no alternative than to visit humanity and intervene in our affairs, desires and demands.

In summary; It is constant non stopping prayers that provoke divine intervention that I call the secret of prevailing prayers. Acts 6:4 But we will give ourselves continually to prayer, and to the ministry of the word. May the Lord find your endurance and patience worthy of speedy intervention, in the name of Jesus. Amen.

4. The Voice of Thanksgiving

Psalm 26:7
"That I may publish with the voice of thanksgiving, and tell of all thy wondrous works."

Next, you will need to understand the secret of thanksgiving. No matter the outcome God, is determined to comfort you, especially if you make thanksgiving your lifestyle.

Isaiah 51:3
For the LORD shall comfort Zion: he will comfort all her waste places; and he will make her wilderness like Eden, and her desert like the garden of the LORD; joy and gladness shall be found therein, thanksgiving, and the voice of melody.

It is time to establish yourself in the kingdom of God by giving thanks always unto God.

Psalms 95:2-3
Let us come before his presence with thanksgiving, and make a joyful noise unto him with psalms. For the LORD is a great God, and a great King above all gods.

Develop the mentality of giving thanks unto God no matter the situation nor the frustration. Thanksgiving is a law and an integral derivative of prevailing in prayer. We are admonished in the bible to learn to give thanks unto God. Otherwise you will provoke a curse and darkness over your life.

Jeremiah 13:16
Give glory to the LORD your God, before he cause darkness, and before your feet stumble upon the dark mountains, and, while ye look for light, he turn it into the shadow of death, and make it gross darkness.

Another interpretation of giving thanks unto God means .that any time you give thanks to God, you are reminding Him how good He is; because you are reminding Him, He will visit your situation with unprecedented and unstoppable speed. Worship proves the holiness of God and that praise provokes the greatness of God, but it is thanksgiving that tells of the goodness of God.

Psalms 107:1-2
O give thanks unto the LORD, for he is good: for

his mercy endureth forever. Let the redeemed of the LORD say so, whom he hath redeemed from the hand of the enemy.

Thanksgiving is a habit that turns into a character and becomes a lifestyle. It is a kingdom mystery that provokes mastery over every affair of your life, no matter the challenge nor the obstacle. Often times, many who give thanks see problems, challenges and obstacles an opportunity to catapult them into their next level. Take a few minutes and give quality thanks unto God first for keeping you alive, secondly, for making you see the light of today and for allowing you to read this heavenly revealed secret.

Remember the story, in Luke 17:15-19, where the Lord Jesus healed ten lepers, but only one leper came back thanking Jesus and glorifying God. Jesus made this one leper whole.

Luke 17:15-19
And one of them, when he saw that he was healed, turned back, and with a loud voice glorified God, And fell down on his face

at his feet, giving him thanks: and he was a Samaritan. And Jesus answering said, Were there not ten cleansed? but where are the nine? There are not found that returned to give glory to God, save this stranger. And he said unto him, Arise, go thy way: thy faith hath made thee whole.

The kingdom mystery definition is that; there is power in thanksgiving. Thanksgiving provokes God to appear on the scene.

Isaiah 30:29-30
Ye shall have a song, as in the night when a holy solemnity is kept; and gladness of heart, as when one goeth with a pipe to come into the mountain of the LORD, to the mighty One of Israel. And the LORD shall cause his glorious voice to be heard, and shall shew the lighting down of his arm, with the indignation of his anger, and with the flame of a devouring fire, with scattering, and tempest, and hailstones. May the God of Jacob remember your heart and accept your thanks, in Jesus' Name. Amen.

5

The Power of Praise

Psalms 21:13
Be thou exalted, LORD, in thine own strength: so will we sing and praise thy power

One great man of God once said that any time prayer fails, try praise. In fact, in between the time you are waiting and exercising patience and endurance on God to intervene on your behalf, allow your high praises to go up to heaven. It is scriptural to develop a lifestyle of praise, especially in times of fervent prayer. We are admonished to use praise as a weapon of deliverance (2 Chronicles 20:20-25).

Psalms 149:6-9
Let the high praises of God be in their mouth, and a two-edged sword in their hand; To execute vengeance upon the heathen, and punishments upon the people; To bind their

kings with chains, and their nobles with fetters of iron; To execute upon them the judgment written: this honour have all his saints. Praise ye the Lord.

Let us recall the miraculous intervention in Acts 16:25-26: *And at midnight Paul and Silas prayed, and sang praises unto God: and the prisoners heard them. And suddenly there was a great earthquake, so that the foundations of the prison were shaken: and immediately all the doors were opened, and every one's bands were loosed.*

Praise is one of the greatest mysteries in the kingdom of God that defends and delivers anyone at the expense of the enemy. Although praise is an instrument of breakthrough and turn around, it is also a weapon of war. Until you offer praise unto God with conviction and understanding, your praise will never be acceptable in the sight of God. To learn more about praise please get a copy of my book on praise titled: Provoking Acceptable Praise.

Briefly let's examine some hindrances

to praise.

Hindrances to Praise

1) Pride: Pride is, without reservation, a great obstacle and a hindrance to your praise unto God. Prides is a hindrance to any great destiny. Jeremiah 13:16-17, Acts 12:22-23
2) Murmuring: As long as you complain and murmur you cannot send quality praise into heaven. 1 Corinthians 10:10
3) Complaining: As long as you continue to complain and nag on what you do not have, God will reject your praise.
4) Disputing: As long as you are always disputing and fighting, you do not belong to this kingdom; God will always hinder your praise. Philippians 2:14
5) Ingratitude: as long as you are never satisfied with the acts of God, God will leave you alone to face your own destruction. Psalms 28:5 says, "Because they regard not the works of the LORD, nor the operation of his hands, he shall destroy them, and not build them up."
6) Greed: A man who is never content is heading into his grave. God can never be

mocked; what you sow is what you will wear and reap. Permit me to put it that way. Godliness with contentment is great gain. 1 Timothy 6:6

Prayer of SALVATION

I am glad you have read this book all the way from the beginning to this point. All I have said, from the beginning, will remain a story until you commit it into practice. When you commit it into practice it becomes a revealed mystery

Before you begin to put it into practice, if you have not done so already, surrender your life to Jesus. I want you to know the truth! The truth is that Jesus died for your sins and, because He died, you must be alive and prosperous.

What must I do to determine my divine visitation? To determine divine visitation you must be born again!

The word says that as many as received him, to them gave He power to become the sons of God; even to them that believe on his name.

To qualify for divine visitation do the following sincerely:
1. Acknowledge that you are a sinner and that He died for you. Romans 3:23
2. Repent of your sins. Acts 3:19, Luke 13:5, 2 Peter 3:9
3. Believe in your heart that Jesus died for your sin. Romans 10:10
4. Confess Jesus as the Lord over your life. Romans 10:10, Acts 2:21

Now repeat this Prayer after me…

Say Lord Jesus, I accept you today, as my Lord and my savior; forgive me of my sins, wash me with your blood. Right now, I believe I am sanctified, saved and free; I am free from the Power of sin to serve the Lord Jesus. Thank you Lord for saving me. Amen. Congratulations: YOU ARE NOW A BORN AGAIN CHRISTIAN. AGAIN I SAY TO YOU CONGRATULATIONS

I adjure you to watch the Spirit of God bear witness with your spirit confirming His word with signs following. The word says that the Spirit itself beareth witness with our spirit, that we are the children of God.

About the Author

Rev Franklin N Abazie is the founding and Presiding Pastor of Miracle of God Ministries with headquarters in Newark, New Jersey USA and a branch church in Owerri- Imo State Nigeria. He is following the footsteps of one of his mentors, Oral Roberts (Healing Evangelist) of the blessed memory. The Lord passed Oral Roberts healing mantle two days before he went to be with the Lord at age 91 into the hand of healing evangelist-Rev Franklin N Abazie in a vision.

In all his services the Power and Presence of God is present to heal all in his audience. He is an ordained man of God with a Healing Ministry reviving the healing and miracle ministry of Jesus Christ of Nazareth.

Pastor Franklin N Abazie, is called by God with a unique mandate: "THE MOMENT IS DUE TO IMPACT YOUR

WORLD THROUGH THE REVIVAL OF THE HEALING & MIRACLE MINISTRY OF JESUS CHRIST OF NAZARETH. I AM SENDING YOU TO RESTORE HEALTH UNTO THEE AND I WILL HEAL THEE OF THY WOUNDS. SAID THE LORD OF HOST"

He is a gifted ardent Teacher of the word of God who operates also in the office of a Prophet, generating and attracting undeniable signs & wonders, special miracles and healings, with apostolic fireworks of the Holy Ghost. He is the founding and presiding senior Pastor of this fast growing Healing ministry. He has written over 86 inspirational, healing and transforming books covering almost all aspect of divine healing and life. He is happily married and blessed with children.

MIRACLE OF GOD HEALING MINISTRIES

Nigeria Healing Crusade 2012
Uli, Anambra State, Nigeria

www.ingramcontent.com/pod-product-compliance
Lightning Source LLC
Chambersburg PA
CBHW052030290426
44112CB00014B/2460